Other titles by John Kinross

Discovering the Smallest Churches in Scotland
Discovering the Smallest Churches in Wales
Discovering the Smallest Churches in England
Discovering the Battlefields of England and Scotland
Discovering Castles in England and Wales

Design: Philip Gray
Typeface: Bembo
Print: SS Media Ltd
Forest Stewardship Council certified paper

Published by Fineleaf Editions, 2012
Moss Cottage, Pontshill, Ross-on-Wye HR9 5TB
www.fineleaf.co.uk   books@fineleaf.co.uk

British Library Cataloguing in Publication Data
A catalogue record for this book is available from the British Library.

Houses with Private Chapels
in the Heart of England

David,
Best wishes, *John*

John Kinross

fineleaf

PUBLISHED BY FINELEAF, ROSS-ON-WYE
www.fineleaf.co.uk

Locations

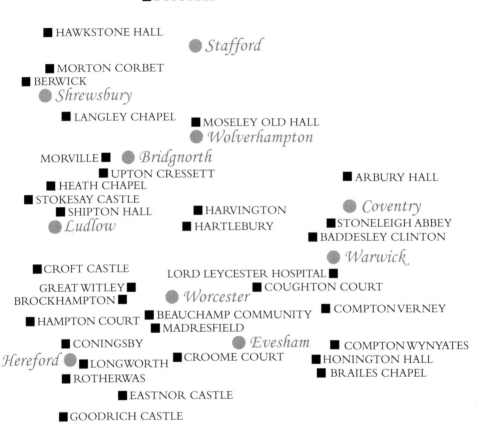

This map gives an indication of approximate locations
and is not drawn to an accurate scale

Contents

Foreword

The partnership of Church and State, sacred and secular, is nowhere better seen than in the great houses of our land, where the religious faith of their incumbents is expressed in some of the most beautiful and unusual places of worship. Owners of these great houses were very aware of their responsibilities not only as landowners and employers but also as leaders in the political and religious life of their day and the places of worship associated with these houses, be it the local parish church or specially commissioned chapels, assumed particular significance.

This whole subject has never been tackled in detail before and we owe John Kinross a great debt of gratitude for bringing these splendid and unusual places of worship to our attention. From the simplicity of Langley Chapel in Shropshire to the baroque splendours of Great Witley, in this book we are introduced to a world almost lost to us today, in which squire and people were united not only in an ordered society but also in the central place occupied by their faith.

I warmly commend this book.

Michael Tavinor
Dean of Hereford

Introduction

What is special about the private chapels in the counties of Herefordshire, Shropshire, Staffordshire, Worcestershire and Warwickshire the reader may well ask? There are the obvious ones like the Roman Catholic chapels that are relics of the intoleration of the sixteenth and seventeenth century rulers who were keen not only to stop the support of the Roman Catholic Church overseas but also to capture the priests. Thus we have Baddlesley Clinton, Harvington, Coughton, Moseley Old Hall and, of course, Boscobel.

Then there are the unusual chapels. Stoneleigh Abbey chapel was built in the 1740's because the owners did not want to worship in the local church but, though not openly Jacobite, they preferred the old services to the new Hanoverian ones. The outstanding chapel at Madresfield was built as a wedding present and decorated with pictures of the family in Arts and Crafts style. There are isolated chapels like Rotherwas, Heath, Brockhampton and Langley where the main house has gone but the chapel remains. Then there are the 'hospitals' of Lord Leycester and Coningsby for old soldiers and the Beauchamp Community for retired clergy and others. Finally, there are the churches next door to large houses, which I have included as most of the family tombs are there – Croome, Shipton, Morville, Honington, the Comptons, Eastnor and of course Great Witley, probably the finest ex-chapel of the collection and now the parish church. One or two like Hawkstone and Moreton Corbet don't come into any real categories but architecturally are worth a visit.

I have left out ones that are so private they are not open to the public but put in others like Hampton Court (used for weddings) and that at Goodrich Castle which is sitting there with stained glass, a nice floor and ceiling but unused since the Civil War. No school or hospital chapels are included. Longworth has recently been taken over by the old convent and the St Michael's Hospice, but still needs further repairs.

Finally, Cobbett in his *Rural Rides* writes about in England in the 1820's. He went to see his friend Hanford on Bredon Hill:

> *The house is of ancient date, and it appears to always have been inhabited by, and the property of Roman Catholics; for there is in one corner of the very top of the building, up in the very roof of it, a Catholic chapel, as ancient as the roof itself. It is about twenty-five feet long and ten wide... At the back of the altar there is a little room ... and adjoining this little room, there is a closet, in which a trap-door made to let the priest down into one of those hiding places, which were contrived for the purpose of evading the grasp of those greedy Scottish minions, to whom that pious and tolerant Protestant, James I, delivered over those English gentlemen, who remained faithful to the religion of their fathers, and, to set his country free, from which greedy and cruel grasp, that honest Englishman, Guy Fawkes, wished as he bravely told the King and his Scotch council, 'to blow the Scotch beggars back to their mountains again ...'*

This book attempts to show that whether Protestant or Catholic, the average Englishman could have his private chapel, priest or minister, and fill his chapel with his friends regardless of who was to call on his door and what was going on in his local church.

John Kinross
Hereford

Acknowledgements

Firstly, I would like to thank Michael Tavinor, Dean of Hereford, for his foreword and for his encouragement; then Bernard Lowry for many of the photographs, Alison Poole for her line drawings and, amongst the house owners, Mrs Bishop, Dr and Mrs Douglas, Bill Cash MP and his son, and the various guides of National Trust and English Heritage properties. Finally, I could not have succeeded without the help of my wife, as well as the photographs she took, and for the careful editing of my publisher. Thanks also to Sallyann who transcribed the original manuscript.

Photographs and drawings

Sources of all illustrations are given on pages 103–104

Arbury Hall

Nuneaton, Near Coventry CV10 7PT
Telephone: 02476 382804
www.arburyestate.co.uk
Owner: Viscount Daventry
Directions: Two miles south west of Nuneaton
Current opening (may vary): House open to groups of 25
or more from Easter to September. Also open Bank Holiday
Sundays and Mondays, Easter to September, 2.00pm to
5.00pm. Tea Room.

A fine example of Gothic Revival architecture, the Hall stands on the site of an Augustinian priory and a later house of 1580. The long gallery still survives on the first floor, but most of the house was 'Gothicised' by Sir Roger Newdegate, who is still known today as the founder of the Newdegate Prize for poetry at Oxford University. Wren did some plans for the entrance portico (unused) and Newdegate Gothicised the house at the same time as Walpole was working at Strawberry Hill. He used Sanderson Miller as his consulting architect, but did much of the work himself. The drawing room and dining room were supervised by Henry Keene and after him a local man, Henry Couchman. The architect, William Hiorn of Warwick, also worked on the library (1754-61) which has an elaborate 'bridge' beam at the Gothic window end to support the curved ceiling. Under it is a minor Gothic beam so that the three Gothic windows have two accentuated lines above, which helps to take the eye off such minor things as the bookshelves. In fact, one has to admit that the books themselves are only a secondary part of the amazing room.

The house is associated with George Eliot, whose father was agent to the estate and she was born here. Both Sir George and his house appear in *Scenes from Clerical Life*. Sir Roger, seventh and youngest son of the third baronet, changed his name to Newdigate and the heiress of Sir Francis, Governor of Western Australia, married the son of Viscountess Daventry (the widow of Captain Fitzroy MP, Speaker of the House of Commons 1928-43), which is how it descended to the Daventry family.

In 1954 the house was threatened by a coal mine, but was reprieved by the then Housing Minister, one Harold Macmillan, a keen member of the Trollope Society and no doubt a reader of George Eliot's *Scenes from Clerical Life,* where the house is called Cheverel Manor.

In 1835 Arbury passed to a great-nephew who assumed the name of Newdigate-Newdegate (two spellings) and became MP for North Warwickshire. His cousin, Lt Gen Sir Edward Newdigate-Newdegate succeeded him, but was not often at home as he was Governor of Bermuda. His nephew, Sir Francis, was MP for Tamworth and later Governor of both Tasmania and later Western Australia. It was Mrs Fitzroy Newdegate who succeeded him in 1936, (the 'e' took over from the 'i' at last!), with her son Humphrey who was ADC to Lord Mountbatten. He played cricket for both Northamptonshire and Warwickshire in the same season (presumably not if one team was playing the other.) It is his son, the fourth Viscount Daventry, who runs the house today.

THE CHAPEL

This was constructed in 1678 in the north-east of the house with a stucco ceiling by Edward Martin (who was paid £48 for it 'besides coming and going and goat's hair') and on the wall are leaf-wreaths supposedly by Gibbons. The floor is of black and white marble squares and the furniture pushed to one side so it is not clear if the room is still used as a chapel.

Baddesley Clinton

Rising Lane, Knowle, Solihull B93 0DQ
Telephone: 01564 783294
www.nationaltrust.org.uk
Owner: The National Trust.
Directions: ¾ mile west of the A4141 Birmingham to Warwick
Road. Two miles away is Packwood House and some visitors
combine the two places for the day. There is a shop and a
restaurant.
Current opening (may vary):
1 January to 10 February, 12.00 to 4.00pm, seven days
11 February to 4 November, 11.00am to 5.00pm, seven days
5 November to 31 December, 12.00 to 4.00pm, seven days

Baddesley Clinton is a moated manor house. 'Baeddi' is a Saxon word for a clearing in the wood or 'Baeddi's Lea'. Originally part of the Hampton-in- Arden manor, it passed to Sir Thomas de Clinton in c.1290 and was henceforward known as Baddesley Clinton. James de Clinton may have built the moat. The De Clintons did not own it for long as it passed through the Coningsby, Dudley, Burdet and Metley families until 1438 when the Warwick lawyer, John Brome, a Lancastrian supporter, purchased it and built most of the house we see today, adding garderobes, the fish ponds and a profitable tile works. He constructed a sewer under the west wing so that even today the moat is reasonably clean. John was killed in 1468 in London by the steward of Warwick the King-maker. The second son, Nicholas, who inherited Baddesley in 1483 avenged his father's death by killing the steward on the Warwick to Barford Road. To expiate this sin and also the murder of the minister of Baddesley Clinton church nearby whom he caught 'tickling his wife under the chin in his own parlour', Nicholas built the steeple of Packwood church and the tower of nearby Baddesley Clinton, St Michael.

When he died in 1517 the house was inherited by his daughter Constance and her husband Sir Edward Ferrers. It has remained in the Ferrers family from that date until acquired by the National Trust in 1980.

It was Henry Ferrers (1549-1651) known as the Antiquary, who with his son Edward (1585-1651) built the south range with the Great Hall, re-modelled the Great Parlour, put in the priest holes and built the chapel and sacristy. This was originally a bedroom with an altar that could be quickly made into an ordinary table when there was trouble. The priests could then get to the sacristy where there was a trap-door leading to the sewer that runs through the kitchen floor (seen by a glass panel today) then a larger room below moat level which the servant of Father Garnet, Nicholas Owen, had fashioned in the same way as the one he had built at Harvington.

There is a remarkable description in Caraman's book *Father Gerard, the Autobiography of an Elizabethan* (1951) of a troubled day at Baddesley Clinton that is worth quoting in full:

About five o'clock the following morning I was making my meditation, Father Southwell was beginning Mass (in the bedroom-cum-chapel) ... when suddenly I heard a great uproar outside the main door. Then I heard a voice shouting and swearing at a servant who was refusing them entrance. It was the priest-hunters or pursuivants as they are called ... there were four of them altogether with swords drawn and they were battering at the door to force an entrance. But a faithful servant held them back, otherwise we should have all been caught.

Father Southwell heard the din. He guessed what it was all about, and slipped off his vestments and stripped the altar bare. While he was doing this, we laid hold of our personal belongings; nothing was left to betray the presence of a priest. Even our boots and swords were hidden away – they would have aroused suspicion if none of the people they belonged to were found. Our beds presented a problem; as they were still warm and ... some of us went off and turned the beds and put the cold side up to delude anyone who put his hand in to feel them.

Baddesley Clinton - Sacristy, or old chapel, by Alison Poole
(note the trapdoor leading to the priest hole)

Outside the ruffians were bawling and yelling, but servants held the door fast. They said that the mistress of the house, a widow, was not yet up, but was coming down at once to answer them. This gave us enough time to stow ourselves and all our belongings into a very cleverly built sort of cave. At last the leopards were let in. They tore madly through the whole house, searched everywhere, pried with candles into the darkest corners. They took four hours over the work but fortunately they chanced on nothing ...

When they had gone, and gone a good way, so that there was no danger of them turning back as they sometimes do, a lady came and called us out of our den, not one but several Daniels. The hiding place was below ground level; the floor was covered with water and I was standing with my feet in it all the time. Father Garnet was there, also Father Southwell and Father Oldcorne (all to be martyrs later), Father Stanney and myself, two secular priests (presumably not Jesuits) and two or three laymen.

They were saved by the priest hole although this episode took place in 1591 and it was the grandson, Henry, who somewhat unwittingly was involved in the Gunpowder Plot a few years later. Henry studied law at Oxford and was a member of the Middle Temple in London in 1572. Ten years later he married Jane White from Hampshire and they moved to London, where Jane died when giving birth to daughter Mary. Henry, always in debt, moved to a house next to the Houses of Parliament. He assigned the lease of this house to Thomas Percy, a friend who also happened to be one of the main plotters of the 1605 Gunpowder Plot. Guy Fawkes used Henry's house to store his powder – which came from the Tower of London, but Henry was by then back at Baddesley Clinton and deplored the plot. He and his son lived in some poverty, and Edward's son, Henry, had to let the park for £60 a year. By the eighteenth century, the estate was run down until Edward Ferrers (1790-1830) and his wife Lady Harriet Townsend moved here. She was the eldest daughter of Lord Townsend, who was also the 16th Baron Ferrers of Tamworth Castle, Staffordshire. Thus the families were re-united after 354 years.

The last of the Ferrers to live here, Marmion, Edward's son, married Rebecca Orpen in the Roman Catholic chapel at Deal, Kent. His best friends were Edward Dering and Lady Chatterton and the four of them came to live at Baddesley Clinton where today many of Rebecca's pictures can be seen in the house. In fact it seems to be as much the house of Rebecca as Manderley was in the mind of its creator Daphne du Maurier.

THE CHAPEL

It was Thomas Ferrers in 1940 (who was really a Walker, but changed his name to Ferrers) who pulled down a staircase and arranged the sacristy as it is today with two and a half windows irregularly placed, an altar, cross and open bible. Thomas also re-arranged Lady Chatterton's chapel with Rebecca's paintings and several family shields to remind the visitors of the need to pray for souls of departed family members. Rebecca lived until 1923 and mass has not been said in the chapel since, but the Ferrers-Walkers, especially Commander Ferrers-Walker RN started to open the house for visitors until, with help from the Mellor Foundation, the National Trust were persuaded to buy it in 1980.

The church of St Michael (not always open, but ask in the house first) is a short walk away. It has a short nave, a tower and was restored in 1872 by Lady Chatterton. The chancel has a screen dated 1634 and there is a tomb-chest to Sir Edward Ferrers and Bridget his wife dated 1564. The wood between the church and the house is noted for its fine bluebells in April.

Beauchamp Community

Newland, Nr Malvern, Worcestershire WR13 5AX
Telephone: 01684 579186 or 01684 562100
Situated on the road to Madresfield, the Community has its
own church. Visitors are welcome throughout the week by
appointment. Please telephone to make arrangements.

The third Earl Beauchamp of Madresfield founded the community for '24 decayed agricultural labourers'. Nowadays it is mostly retired clergy who live here, not just in the almshouses but in the Pyndar Court wing (1986) and East wing, which is Victorian. There is a library, a mortuary chapel (Hopkins, 1865) and a warden's lodge. There was once a timber church with a burial ground: now the site has a large cross (1866) by Hardwick who built the present church used as the community chapel, and dedicated to St Leonard.

ST LEONARD'S CHURCH

The church is noted for its elaborate wall paintings covering most of the walls. The one above the chancel arch is by Preedy (one of the few Victorian architects who was also a stained glass window artist) showing the Last Judgement (1865) and others show the miracle of the loaves and fishes, raising of Lazarus, Good Samaritan, Talents, Beatitudes and many other biblical scenes. The Nave roof has paintings of chains (St Leonard is the patron saint of prisoners). There is a four bay arcade between chancel and nave, and a brass to Earl Beauchamp, brought here from Preedy's Madresfield Church. Not to everyone's taste, the church is used regularly by the community and kept in good condition. For those who do like this style it is worth seeing the Parry wall paintings at Higham Court in Gloucestershire. This stands next to a fine garden which is open to the public, (see the *Yellow Book*), so there are compensations.

Berwick Chapel

Pimhill, Shropshire SY4 3HW
Owner: Mr and Mrs A James
Current opening (may vary): Most Sunday mornings at
11.00am for a service. The chapel, which is not part of the
local parochial church, is two miles north of Shrewsbury in a
bend of the River Severn on a private estate.

Completely surrounded by cattle, this is a building more interesting on the
inside than the outside. Built in 1672 (the tower much later) for Sir Samuel
Jones, a chancel was added by Osborn in 1892. There are box pews, a west
gallery and much wooden panelling and the Royal Arms of George III. There

Berwick Chapel

is a fine wagon roof in the chancel. Jones also built some almshouses nearby (see below) and Berwick House dates from 1731 with many Victorian alterations. It was built for Thomas Powys. In the nineteenth century it belonged to James Watson MP, whose heiress married into the Phillips family. One window commemorates Reginald Phillipps (d.1915) and on the porch wall is a tablet to William Molton, 'an honest and good man', born 1703, d.1803. There are hatchments to the Powys family in the chapel as well as a standing figure of a girl reading, the provenance of which Mr Leonard states is unknown.

Sir Samuel Jones built sixteen almshouses in a rectangular site between the church and the road. They are in good condition and date from 1672, approached on the fourth side of the rectangle by a stone arch rather like a fort. There are some splendid diagonal chimneys and each has a small garden behind. Modern builders please note.

Boscobel House

Bishop's Wood, Brewood, Staffordshire ST1 9AR
Telephone: 01902 850244   www.english-heritage.org.uk
Owner: English Heritage
Directions: 8 miles north of Wolverhampton on an
unclassified road between A5 and A41.
Current opening (may vary): April to October, Wednesday
to Sunday and Bank Holiday Mondays, 10.00am to 5.00pm.
No café but picnics welcome.

Boscobel House will forever be associated with Charles II's escape after the Battle of Worcester when he hid in an oak tree. It was built in 1630 by John Giffard, son of Edward Giffard of White Ladies – now a ruined priory – a mile away and also owned by English Heritage. The Giffards were Roman Catholics and there are two priest holes in the house as well

Boscobel House, 1930, by William A Green *(opposite)*

as a room known as The Oratory where a priest could take a service for the owner and his family. In 1712, William Stukely, the antiquary, visited Boscobel and said the chapel was in the garret or attic and that there was a cavity with a trap-door entrance over the staircase where the royal guest spent the night.

Off the squire's bedroom is a closet with a trapdoor and another priest hole only 2 feet 3 inches high which much have been very uncomfortable.

CHARLES'S ESCAPE

After being certain the Battle of Worcester (1651) was lost, Charles left the town in the dark on 3rd September with Lord Wilmot and a few others going north where they were joined by some Scottish cavalry. Giffard, who was present, took the King to White Ladies and here the Penderel brothers guided him to Boscobel. He had disguised himself as a peasant by then, had his hair cut, and face blackened by soot.

At first he thought of crossing the Severn and going to Swansea to find a ship for France. Warned that all river crossings were closely watched, he turned back and made for Boscobel. Here he found Major Carless, another escapee from the battle. He was given some bread and cheese, slept in the attic priest's hole and then went outside to hide in the great oak tree with Major Careless all day while Cromwell's men searched the wood.

Two days later he was at Moseley, home of Thomas Whitgreave, en route for Bristol and eventually getting to Sussex where he was ferried across to France, in the *Surprise*, a coal brig, on 15th October. The houses at both White Ladies and Boscobel were closely searched and the Penderels closely questioned but not arrested. The only man to suffer was Francis Yates who had guided him to White Ladies after his attempt to cross the Severn. He was captured and executed in Oxford.

Boscobel farmyard circa 1910

Brailes Chapel

Friars Lane, Lower Brailes, Warwickshire OX15 5JQ
Directions: On the B4035 between Shipton-on-Sour and Banbury.

The village is divided into Upper and Lower Brailes. The chapel is part of a farm complex in Upper Brailes and is on a first floor in an unlikely outbuilding. It dates from the early 17th century, when Roman Catholic chapels were few in the country and had to be well-hidden. In the Manor House next door lived William Bishop, a Roman Catholic priest and later a bishop, but he was under constant threat of disclosure and his house has a hiding place in the attic. The chapel has an original seventeenth century communion rail, seating for about 40 and some vestments of the same date given by the Sheldon family, who were tapestry weavers.

Brailes is famous for two other things. Firstly, in the 1920's it was the scene of an outbreak of diphtheria which killed 37 children. Their monument is in the church.

On a happier note, Brailes was the home of William de Brailes who was an artist in the thirteenth century responsible for some very fine illuminated manuscripts, some of which are in the Fitzwilliam Museum, Cambridge. As well as painting manuscripts, Brailes was also a designer of vestments so he may well have been a Roman Catholic supporter of the local priest.

BRAILES CHAPEL

The Roman Catholic chapel of Lower Brailes is close to St George's church down a lane with a new car park. When you get there it is still difficult to see the chapel. This is because it is upstairs in the building to the right of the presbytery. There is a steep stair to it to the right of the front door of the presbytery. This was once a malt barn, but in 1726 it was one of the earliest non-Reformation Catholic chapels in England. Father Bishop, a relation of William Bishop, was a Catholic scholar who was appointed first Bishop of Chalcedon in Paris (1623).

When we called there were a set of seventeenth and eighteenth century vestments on show – which are still used on special occasions. The other vestments and plate are kept in Oscott College, Birmingham but the chapel has part of a candlestick supposed to have belonged to King Charles II – tradition says he held it when being converted by Father Huddleston on his deathbed.

The blue painted panelling is original, the unusual windows with coloured crosses are later and the organ (1826) came to the chapel four years ago. At the same time the icon of St Peter & St Paul was given to the chapel as it is dedicated to them. In the presbytery there is a priest's hiding place and beneath the chapel the old kitchen is now a meeting hall.

Brailes is a delightful spot to find and the priest's vegetable garden next door is magnificent.

External stairs leading to Brailes Chapel

Brailes Chapel interior

Brockhampton-by-Bromyard

New Chapel, Brockhampton Estate, Bringsty,
Worcestershire WR6 5TB
Directions: Two miles east from Bromyard off the A44. On the
lane to Lower Brockhampton, a National Trust property which
has a tea shop and car park.
Current opening (may vary): Bank Holiday afternoons, also
before and after services on fourth Sunday afternoons.

The Barneby family, owners of Brockhampton Park, tired of using the
Norman chapel (now ruined) next to the moated manor house (NT) at
Lower Brockhampton, built the new chapel in 1798. Its architect was
George Byfield, better known for designing prisons. He designed it in
Gothic Revival style, not to be confused with Shobdon's Strawberry Hill
Gothic which is 'over the top' in comparison with the restraint of Byfield.

The Barneby family, who sometimes called themselves Lutleys, wanted
a family chapel and all monuments inside are to members of the family.
The chapel is a Free Church Donative, so that on the death of Colonel
Barneby in 1946 a monthly service was authorised but the chapel was
vested in its congregation. It has very regular congregations and all clergy
expenses are paid by the diocese.

The stained glass is worthy of attention. The original three light
window by Eginton (c.1810) is meant to be the Transfiguration with a lot
of red paint. It is to be restored when enough funds have been raised. The
shortage of red glass due to the Napoleonic wars meant Eginton used red
paint – a good example of his craft can be seen at Birmingham Museum.
The east window (where once the Eginton stood) is Faith, Hope and
Charity with St Cecilia holding a portable organ with the pipes falling
out. This is by Mary Lowndes (1886) who later became well known for

painting banners for the suffragette movement. The south windows (there are none on the north face apart from a single light in the vestry) are by Ada Curry (1891) and show the virtues of Humility, Truth, Purity and Patience. The last named is a lady holding her 'bulge' and spreading her bare feet, pregnant – an unusual picture in stained glass. There are some good monuments, one to Lydia Bulkeley (1812) by John Bacon (Junior) being very fine and the mosaic reredos by Lowndes is quite striking.

With its chapel seating like a university college and a gallery it is easy to imagine the Colonel's maids forming the choir (whether or not they could sing) and the service going in military style. One of his forebears, it states, was responsible for 'improving prison discipline' so that is probably why George Byfield was the chosen architect.

Brockhampton-by-Bromyard Chapel, by Alison Poole

them in South Wales, he often stayed with John Barneby at the 'Big House'. This would account for several 'Arch features.

Compton Verney

Compton Verney, Warwickshire CV35 9HZ
Telephone: 01926 645500
www.comptonverney.org.uk
Owners: Compton Verney House Trust
Directions: On the B4086 between Kineton and
Wellesbourne; nine miles east of Stratford-on-Avon
Current opening (may vary): End March to December,
Tuesday to Sunday and Bank Holiday Mondays, 11.00am
to 5.00pm. Groups welcome. Last entry 4.30pm.
Cafe and toilets.

Compton Verney, now an art gallery with two or three different exhibitions
a year, is an imposing house by a large lake. The original house dates from
1714 and a was built for George Verney, Lord Willoughby de Broke who
was Dean of Windsor. It has a Vanbrugh appearance but the architect is not
known. The 14th Earl called in Adam to extend the south side and later
Capability Brown designed the bridge, the grounds and the chapel. Pevsner
thinks Adam's alterations make the house rather dull. Further alterations were
made in 1855 by Gibson, who made a coffered ceiling and frieze in Adam's
portico. The interior had Zucchi panels (1766) and was altered by Lord
Manton who purchased the house from the Verneys in 1921. Windows were
lowered and the whole interior character of the house altered.

THE CHAPEL

Originally there was a church near the lake but this was demolished and
Brown erected the rectangular box chapel in 1772. The interior, which is
to be opened to the public in 2012, is more Adam in style than anything

else in the house. It has a west gallery, chapel-like seating, three-decker pulpit and monuments to members of the Verney family, many moved from the old church. There is a fine Westmacott monument to Lady Lewisham (1798) and some ledger stones of black marble and brass. Mee says that he was taken by the brass of Richard Verney's sister, Anne, in her veil, gown and petticoat with her hands at prayer. There is also one of George Verney showing his flowing hair, moustache and armour. Mee, writing in 1936, says the chapel ceased to be used but at least if it is opening again in 2012 it is a start, even if most of the stained glass is now in the USA.

Compton Wynyates

Compton Wynyates House, Tysoe, Warwickshire CV35 0UD
Owner: Marquis of Northampton

The house is not open to the public, although it used to be in the 1960's and perhaps will be again, one hopes. I can recall the great hall, some fine needlework pictures, a carved panel showing the English and French knights at the Battle of Tournay (1513) and a picture of the first Earl of Shrewsbury who fought against Joan of Arc.

The house lies in a hollow, built of pink brick, with a squat battlemented porch, many twisted chimneys and an air of peace, even though it has had a turbulent past in the Civil War. The second Earl, Spencer Compton, was a supporter of King Charles I and raised a troop of horse for his King, making his four sons officers. He took part in the raising of the siege of Stafford, but at the Battle of Hopton Heath (1643), his troop advanced too far and the Earl was killed, being brought home for burial by his sons. The most junior son, Henry, later became Bishop of London and was responsible for crowning King William III and Queen Mary II. The moat was filled in, in the late seventeenth century.

During the family's absence at war, the house was used as a Parliamentary barracks and the church was ransacked, the alabaster monuments to previous Comptons being thrown into the moat. It was John Berrill who restored things and after the war the third Earl rebuilt the church – outside the house – and the chapel in the house which Pevsner states 'needs no comment'.

THE CHURCH

To the north of the house, it has been rebuilt in 1655, with twin naves, two east windows and many mutilated monuments to the Comptons. There are box pews, font (seventeenth century) an eighteenth century set of communion rails, 17 hatchments and a pulpit between two south windows. The Comptons obtained a marquessate in 1812 and in 1867 much repair work was done by Sir Matthew Digby Wyatt, but none of it destroys the great charm of this house and church.

Coningsby Hospital

Widemarsh Street, Hereford HR4 9HN
Current opening (may vary): Occasionally to the public.
Details from Discover Herefordshire Centre, 1 King Street,
Hereford HR4 9BW. Telephone 01432 268430

Sir Thomas Coningsby of Hampton Court was a friend of Sir Philip Sydney, and a soldier who was Muster Master to the Earl of Essex on his military expedition to Normandy in 1591. He was knighted at Rouen with others, including the young Thomas Fairfax, and as MP for Hereford and Sheriff he was on the council of the Marches under Lord Compton. He was determined to do something for the old soldiers, many of whom had neither food nor shelter. In Widemarsh Street there was a former hostelry and chapel of the Knights Hospitallers of St John of Jerusalem.

Coningsby coat of arms, 1597 (opposite)

In 1614, he purchased this and erected 12 dwellings with a renovated chapel for 'Coningsby's Company of Old Servitors'. The original deed is still extant and provides food and accommodation for 'eleven poor old servitors that have been soldiers, mariners or serving men of seven years' service in one family', one of the said servitors, a soldier, to be Corporal of Coningsby's Company. The Chaplin was deputy head after the Corporal.

Stipends were laid down as: Chaplain, £20; Corporal, £20; ,the Men, £13 each, £130 a year; balance in clothing, £30. Sir Thomas paid £200 a year for his men and they were given a red cloak, uniform, seats in the cathedral and strict rules of behaviour.

The Arkwrights took over the running of the Hospital after Coningsby's sale of Hampton Court and there is an entry in their records of a special Christmas meal in 1851:

This being Old Xmas Day (3 January) went down to Hereford and gave the Corporal and Servitors of Coningsby Hospital a dinner of roast beef and plum pudding at Mr Arkwright's expense and their wives 1/4lb of tea each.

Arkwrights kept the building in good repair and recently the architects, Hook Mason of Hereford, have repaired the fabric so that the Hospital is in good shape.

THE CHAPEL

Upstairs in the north wing, the small chapel has a trussed-rafter roof. The east window glass, three lancets, comes from the disused chapel at Harewood End off the A49 between Ross and Hereford. In the north window are the arms of Coningsby impaling Fitzwilliam, dated 1614. There is a seventeenth century pulpit with carvings and on the west wall is a stone panel containing the Coningsby coat of arms, 1597. The chapel seats at least twenty and is used from time to time, services being taken by local clergymen including the Dean of Hereford.

Coningsby Chapel exterior and interior

Coughton Court

Alcester, Warwickshire B49 5JA
Owner: The National Trust   www.nationaltrust.org.uk
Telephone: 01789 762435 / 400777
Directions: Coughton is on the A435 near Alcester.
Current opening (may vary):
10 March to 25 March, 11.00am to 5.00pm, Saturday, Sunday
31 March to 30 June, 11.00am to 5.00pm, Wednesday to Sunday
1 July to 31 August, 11.00am to 5.00pm, Tuesday to Sunday
1 to 30 September, 11.00am to 5.00pm, Wednesday to Sunday
4 October to 4 November, 11.0am to 5.00pm, Thu to Sun.

Coughton Court is the family home of the Throckmortons, who look after the garden (opening times as house). Guide dogs only. Restaurant, shop and plants for sale.

The house is famous for its gatehouse with two upper rooms and turrets dating from the early sixteenth century. Originally moated, the moat was filled in when the 1688 hall range was taken down so now there are north and south wings as the gatehouse faces west. There were further alterations in 1780 and again in 1835. The family were Catholic servants of the Tudors, Sir John being Under-Treasurer of England and his grandson Robert on the Privy Council of Henry VII. However, the Throckmortons fortunately were not involved in the Gunpowder Plot though Thomas's nephew was Robert Catesby, the chief plotter. The women of the family waited in the drawing room for the outcome of the plot and in the left turret window are the two coats of arms of the Catesby and Tresham families. A daughter married Edward Arderne, who was executed for his involvement in a plot against Elizabeth I. Strangely, on a wall in the passage is a typed copy of the abdication speech of Edward VIII. The family is also related to the Actons. Lady Acton married Sir John, who was also her uncle, when she was 14 and he was 63. He became Prime Minister of Naples and died in 1811, but she lived on at Coughton until 1873.

THE CHAPEL

This stood at the east end of the south wing where the Long Hall is now situated with a staircase removed from Harvington Hall. The house has two priest holes but, unlike Harvington, no interior chapel as the family commissioned Hansom to build a separate church in 1857, close to the parish church with, as Pevsner puts it, an 'unfortunate' turret and some good Hardman stained glass.

The interesting Throckmorton monuments are in the parish church, St Peters, where there is a tomb chest for Sir Robert, who died in the Holy Land in 1518. It was used by a later Sir Robert who died in 1791. In the chancel is Sir George and his wife and children with three brasses of 1533.

The other chancel tombs are to Sir Robert, died 1570 and Sir John who died in 1580. Finally in 1862 Sir Robert and his wife were buried in the chancel in a black marble tomb with a brass and enamel cross.

The guide book has a photograph of the family taken in 1997 – eight adults and five children – so by the time this book appears there may be yet more Throckmortons.

Croft Castle

Yarpole, Herefordshire HR6 9PW   Telephone: 01568 780246
Owner: The National Trust   www.nationaltrust.org.uk
Current opening (may vary) - castle by tour only from
10.00am to 1.00pm:
11 February to 19 February, 10.00am to 4.30pm, seven days
3 March to 4 November, 10.00am to 5.00pm, seven days
10 November to 16 December, 10.00am to 4.30pm, Saturday
and Sunday only. 17th December to 23rd December, 10.00
to 16.30, seven days. Open Bank Holiday Mondays. Shop,
restaurant and walled garden. Park closes at dusk.

Croft Castle is not really a castle, it is a seventeenth century family home with corner turrets. The first Croft, Bernard de Croft, is recorded as the owner in the Domesday Book. His castle was west of the present building and no stones remain. The next Croft, Sir John, married one of the daughters of Owain Glyndwr, so a wounded black dragon appears on their coat-of-arms. Sir Richard Croft, who with his wife Eleanor lies in state in the church next door, was a soldier throughout the Wars of the Roses, helping to put Edward IV on the throne. He then survived the accession of King Henry VII in spite of being involved in Henry's grandfather's execution in Hereford after the Battle of Mortimer's Cross (1461). His great grandson, Sir James Croft, was Queen Elizabeth I's

Comptroller of the Household, looking after the royal finances, and earned enough money to build a small Elizabethan house of the site of Bernard's Castle. He lived to a good age and his son was MP for Leominster. Sir Herbert Croft (1566-1629) married a wealthy heiress and built the shell of the present house, before retiring to a monastery in France, leaving Croft to be run by his three sons. The eldest Sir William became a prisoner of the Parliamentarians in 1642 and two years later Croft was ransacked by Irish troops, brought over by the Royalists, who had not been paid enough. William was killed escaping from a skirmish at Stokesay (described later) and his brother James, a colonel and bachelor, took over but preferred to stay in London. Finally, Herbert, the youngest, who was made Bishop of Hereford, 1661-1691, built the present house.

His son married Elizabeth Archer and she bore him eleven children, of whom only six survived her. This Croft became the first Baronet, and his son Sir Archer Croft was one of the speculators who lost a fortune in the South Sea Bubble. In spite of becoming Governor of New York, a place he never visited, and being given a pension of £1000 a year by Walpole, he sold Croft to his neighbour, Richard Knight of Downton. Richard purchased Croft for his daughter and her Welsh husband, Thomas Johnes. It was Johnes and his wife who employed Thomas Pritchard of Shrewsbury to redecorate the castle in Strawbery Hill Gothic, probably influenced by his neighbour Viscount Bateman at Shobdon (whose church is well known for its Gothic decoration). However, their son, also Thomas, preferred to live in Wales and built a large expensive house at Hafod which caught fire in 1807. The new owner of Croft was a wealthy Ludlow mercer, Somerset Davies, who let the house out as he preferred to live in Ludlow. Herbert Kevill-Davies was killed in World War I (his monument is in the church) and Sir Herbert Croft's son, another Herbert, was killed at Gallipoli.

In 1923, the Crofts, then living at Lugwardine Court, Hereford, offered £30,000 for the castle which was accepted so they moved back into their old family home. Sir James, the 11th Baronet, was a commando in World War II and after surviving the Norway campaign was unfortunately killed

Croft Castle (opposite)

training in Scotland in 1941. His father, now childless, bequeathed Croft to his cousin, Sir Henry Page Croft, first Lord Croft, who was a Tory politician in the House of Lords. During the war the house was occupied by a convent school so was much run down. Diana Uhlman, Lord Croft's sister, did all she could to save the castle and with the help of the National Trust they have succeeded. Two members of the family still live in one wing of the house and much of the walled garden is looked after by volunteers.

THE CHURCH

St Michael's Church next to the castle is still used as a member of the Yarpole parishes today. The building is thirteenth century and similar in design to St Margaret's in the Golden Valley although the nave and chancel are about the same size as each other.

There are box pews, a west gallery, and an altar ceiling that used to be painted with stars and clouds. Perhaps it is time they were restored? The bell turret is in fine condition and the Croft monuments are worth noting, especially that of Sir Richard, dressed in his Wars of the Roses armour, with his wife next to him. There is a blocked up door behind the tomb, which was moved from a small north chapel into the chancel in 1800. The grounds have some ancient trees, a walled garden and some of the best views in the county.

Croome Court

Near High Green, Worcestershire WR8 9DW Tel: 01905 371090
Owner: The National Trust www.nationaltrust.org.uk
Directions: 9 miles south of Worcester, signposted from A38 and B4084. Nearest town is Upton-Upon-Severn.
Current opening (may vary):

St Michael's Church Coft Castle

1 January to 12 February, 11.00 to 4.00, Saturday and Sunday
13 February to 2 November, 11.00 to 4.30pm, daily (not Tuesdays)
3 November to 23 Dec., 11.00 to 4.00pm, Saturady and Sunday
26 December to 31 Dec. 11.00 to 4.00pm, daily except Tuesday
Park, shop and canteen open same days, but open and
close 30 minutes earlier.

This is the home of the Earls of Coventry, and it was the sixth Earl who took
what was a smaller house of the 1640's to the architect Sanderson Miller,
who recommended his landscape gardener friend Lancelot Brown. Miller's
design of Hagley Hall is probably what Brown used as his inspiration, but
Hagley is on a hill and has different chimneys to Croome, so he must
have used some of his own ideas. The house was always an expensive
home for the family and after World War II, when it was occupied by the
RAF (the tea room today is decked out as a 1940 RAF hut), the estate was
sold in 1948 to the Catholic Archdiocese of Birmingham with 38 acres.

They turned it into a boys' school and the lockers are still in the basement, close to the boilers, so probably the warmest part of the house in winter. In 1979 it was sold again to the Hare Krishna, who had a Hindu school here which lasted until 1984. Subsequent owners have had a restaurant, a training centre and a private house, with a huge bath installed over the entrance (still there until just recently). Most of the 5,000 acres were sold off to the farming tenants.

The most attractive room today is the Gallery, designed by Robert Adam in 1760, although the Tapestry Room was removed to the Metropolitan Museum in New York and the bookcases from the library are in the Victoria and Albert Museum. The gallery had ten statues in niches, all classical themes, and still has a fine garlanded fireplace with caryatids; also worth seeing, a triple-panelled ceiling with paintings by Vassalli in the Saloon. (Francesco Vassalli is also credited with working under Pritchard at Shipton.)

THE CHURCH

This is some distance from the house, built by Brown with an Adam interior in 1759-60. As Pevsner says, it is Gothic outside and Georgian Gothic inside. There is a black and white floor and delicate ceilings by Joseph Rose, who did much work in the Court. The early Coventrys are here, a tomb by Stone of the first Baron, who died in 1639; Mary, his daughter-in-law, who died in 1634; Marshall's tomb of her husband who died in 1661; and John, fourth Baron, who died in 1687 by Grinling Gibbons; a tomb from St Martin-in-the-Fields of Hon. Henry Coventry, who died in 1686 and the eighth Earl has his hatchment on the east wall of the north aisle. Finally, the ninth Earl who died in 1930, has his monument here. Since 1975, the building has belonged to the Churches Conservation Trust.

Eastnor Castle

Nr Ledbury, Herefordshire HR8 1RL   Telephone: 01531 633160
www.eastnorcastle.com
Owner: J Hervey-Bathurst
Directions: SE of Ledbury, on the A438 Tewkesbury Road
Current opening (may vary): Easter weekend, Bank Holidays
in May and Sundays, 5th June to 25th September, 11.00am
to 5.00pm. Last entry 4.30pm. Groups welcome.
Weddings. Ice cream parlour, teas and shop. Guides.
Coaches: phone in advance.

Built in 1812 by Sir Robert Smirke for Earl Somers, the Second Baron, whose fortune had been made when his great-grandfather married the heiress of King William III's Lord Chancellor. He was encouraged by his wealthy wife, Margaret, daughter of a well-known antiquarian, Dr Treadway Nash. The castle is Norman Revival in style, with a huge central hall. The Drawing Room was designed by Pugin (1851) and much of the interior is in Gothic style. The Drawing Room has an amazing painted ceiling and fireplace. It contains a portrait of Mrs Fitzherbert, friend of the Prince Regent, whose niece married into the Bathurst family. The library and great hall were decorated by Mr Fox and the woodwork, made in Italy, was assembled on site by local workman. There is another library combined with a billiard room next door.

Upstairs the portrait of the sixth Lady Somers, by De Laszlo, bears a striking resemblance to Penelope Keith. In the Octagon Room is a glass case devoted to Lady Somers who was President of the Temperance Society and in 1913 was voted by the London Evening News as the best candidate for becoming Britain's next Prime Minister. What she thought about this is unknown, especially as women did not have the vote at that time.

Eastnor is the only house I know with two libraries, which would please Virginia Woolf's mother (niece of the third countess) who married Leslie Stephen. In the grounds, apart from the deer park, there is an obelisk to the Hon. Edward Cocks, son of the second Baron, who was killed at Burgos in 1812. The sixth Baron became Chief Scout and when he died in 1944 his daughter Elizabeth married Major Hervey-Bathurst whose son and family run the house and estate today.

THE CHAPEL

This is on the first floor, seats 22, has Victorian stained glass and Jacobean-style panelling. It was given by the daughters of the third Earl and his wife when a bedroom was made into the chapel in the 1880's. There is a painting over the altar by di Antonio and a Madonna and Child by an unknown fourteenth century artist. The chapel has never been consecrated but is used for family prayers. Most of the family tombs are in the local church dedicated to St John which, although the tower is fourteenth century, was 'over-restored' by Sir Giles Gilbert Scott in 1852.

Eastnor castle

Goodrich Castle

Castle Lane, Goodrich, Ross on Wye, Herefordshire HR9 6HY
Owner: English Heritage
www.english-heritage.org.uk
Directions: On the River Wye a few miles south-east of
Ross-on-Wye, the castle is approached by a lane clearly
marked from the centre of the village.
Current opening (may vary):
1 April to 30 June, daily 10.00am to 5.00pm
1 July to 31 Augus, daily 10.00am to 6.00pm
1 September to 3 October, daily 10.00am to 5.00pm
1 November to 28 February, Wednesday to Sunday, 10.00 to 4.00pm
1 March to 31 March, Wednesday to Sunday, 10.00 to 5.00pm
Closed: 24th to 26th December and 1st Jane
Dogs on leads. Children must be supervised as some of the
ruins are hazardous. Cafe and car park.

The castle has a Norman keep but the curtain walling is thirteenth
century. The gatehouse houses the repaired chapel of which more later.
The probable founder of the castle was Godric Mapsonne, who held land
at Howle in Walford. In Norman times it belonged to William Marshall,
Earl of Pembroke who obtained it via his wife, who was the Clare heiress
from South Wales. This was confirmed by King John in 1203. Trusted
by John, the Earl was made guardian of the young prince, Henry III. His
effigy is in the Temple Church, London, together with two of his sons,
William and Gilbert. They were Knights Templar and loyal to the crown.
However, after the death of Anselm, the youngest of the Earl's sons, the
castle passed to the eldest daughter who married Warin de Munchensi.
Their son joined Simon de Montfort so the castle was granted by Henry

III to his half-brother William de Valence (1247). Because of his success at Evesham (1265) in defeating Simon, de Valence (d.1296) was buried in Westminster Abbey. His widow lived at Goodrich for many years and was noted for her charity to the poor. Her son, an opponent of Piers Gaveston, was murdered in 1323 when in France so the castle passed to his niece, Elizabeth Comyn and her husband Richard Talbot. It was this Talbot who strengthened the castle, using money obtained from ransoming his many French prisoners. He founded the Priory at Flanesford and his son fought in France with the Black Prince. His grandson was the famous Sir John Talbot, Earl of Shrewsbury, who won no less than 40 battles before being killed, sword in hand, at the age of 80 at Chatillon (1453). His son was killed in the Battle of Northampton, when Yorkists defeated Lancastrians (1460) and the castle once more reverted to the Earls of Pembroke, only this time the Herberts not the Marshalls.

The Talbots managed to regain the castle and in 1616 Elizabeth Talbot and her husband Henry Grey, Earl of Kent, were here. During the Civil War the castle, at first Royalist, was fortified by Sir Henry Lingen with a small garrison. In 1646, Colonel Birch and Colonel Kyrle marched with 500 men from Hereford and attacked in the dark. They set fire to a hay store, captured some horses but did not capture the castle until more arms and the huge mortar had been set in place. Colonel League described the action:

> Colonel (Birch) made his approaches and mined with all his speed that the cragginess of the place would permit, and not only plied them with his Batteries, but had done very good execution upon the castle with the 'Granados' shot from our Mortar peice.

Sir Henry finally surrendered (31 July, 1646) and Colonel Birch marched the Governor and 50 gentlemen and 120 soldiers to imprisonment in Hereford. Sir Henry and some of his gentlemen were later moved to Red Castle in Montgomery, the ruins of which still stand.

An artist's impression of the chapel in 1500 *(opposite)*

The castle was then slighted and became uninhabitable but continued in the Grey family until the death of Henry, Duke of Kent, in 1740 when it passed to Vice-Admiral Griffin, whose family eventually passed it to the Ministry of Works, now known as English Heritage.

THE CHAPEL

The castle chapel came to life when the Bishop of Hereford dedicated the Millennium Window designed by Nicola Hopwood on 10th June, 2000. It states 'Upon this Rock' and shows the meandering River Wye and how it is linked with the three parishes of Goodrich, Marstow and Welsh Bicknor. In strategic places are the heads of a man, a woman and a child in the river: outlined in white are various children's drawings. The other window was put up in 1992 in memory of eleven crew of a Halifax aircraft, carrying members of the Radar Research Establishment in Malvern, that crashed near here in 1942. Illustrated are all the different elements of radar that made such a contribution to the Battle of Britain.

There is also a display showing a drawing of an artist's impression of the chapel in 1500, when there were nine priests or clerks and 200 people in the castle. The Talbot family has a wooden private pew butting out on the left hand wall, where the steps to it are still intact. There was a rood beam from this to the other wall supported by diagonal struts from the two remaining corbels. The guards could still keep an eye on who was entering the castle through the slit window in the gatehouse wall and the hole for the door drawbar is still there. When open, the bar must have come into the chapel. Perhaps the time will come when the chapel can be re-opened again – all it needs is a few simple furnishings and one more slit window to be glazed.

The Nicola Hopwood window, Goodrich Castle Chapel (*opposite*)

Great Witley Court

Great Witley, Worcestershire WR6 6JT
Telephone 01299 896636
www.english-heritage.org.uk
Directions: 10 miles north west of Worcester off A443.
Owners: English Heritage - the church is not owned by
English Heritage, but is a local parish church today. Tea
shop is next to the church and is independent.
Current opening (may vary):
April to June, daily, 10.00 to 5.00pm
July to end August, 10.00am to 6.00pm
September to end October, 10.00am to 5.00pm
November to February, Wednesday to Sunday, 10.00am to
4.00pm (Closed Christmas)
March, Wednesday to Sunday, 10.00am to 5.00pm

Although a ruin, Witley Court is the former home of the Foleys and later
the Dudleys. Lady Foley paid for the present church to be erected and
the old one demolished in 1735. In 1837 the Ward family, Earls of Dudley,
acquired the Court and during their time it became one of the most
fashionable houses in Britain. In 1843 Queen Adelaide, widow of King
William IV, came to live here. Samuel Daukes was employed to enlarge
the house, case it in Bath stone and re-fashion the interior in French
Renaissance style. Before this Nash had worked on the north and south
porticos, turning what had been an 'H-planned' Jacobean house (only the
bachelor wing remains of this today) into what it was before the terrible
fire of 1937. The grounds were designed by Nesfield and today English
Heritage have restored most of them, including the amazing Perseus
and Andromeda statue, which comes on every half hour when the house

Great Witley Court

Great Witley Church (former chapel) - interior opposite

is open. Carpet businessman Herbert Smith obtained the Court in the 1920's and it was in 1937 that what started as a small kitchen fire turned Witley into a ruin.

THE CHURCH

Lady Foley petitioned for the old church to be taken down and the new one, in a place nearer the house, possibly designed by Gibbs, is an inspiration even today. In 1747, Lord Foley, an ironmaster, obtained the windows, ceiling paintings and organ case from Lord Chandos, who had come into financial problems, and demolished his house and chapel at Cannons in Edgware, London. No expense was spared, special packing cases were made and the ceiling consists of papier mache moulds, as the original plaster would have been too difficult to transport from London. The font was carved by James Nesfield Forsyth, the pews came from an Oxford Street, London shop and all ironwork was made by Foley's craftsmen. When he died, Lord Foley's monument was made by Rysbrack and equals that to the Duke of Marlborough at Blenheim Palace in grandeur.

The stained glass windows were designed by an Italian artist but made between 1719-21 by Joshua Price with enamel painting on glass which look as good today as they must have done in the eighteenth century. The Cannons chapel windows were a bit longer than those at Witley so a gold coloured border had to be added at the foot of each one. They represent the life of Christ in chronological sequence. In the 1970's and in 1993-4 the church was completely restored with help from English Heritage and for those of you who want to see a little more than a ruin, a fine garden and a working fountain, then the church is well worth a long visit.

Great Witley Court Church ceiling detail (opposite)

Hampton Court

Hope-under-Dinmore, Hereford HR6 OPN
Telephone: 01568 79777   www.hamptoncourt.org.uk
Owners: Mr and Mrs Daley
Directions from Hereford: Take the A49 north and after the
Queenswood Hill, pass Hope-under-Dinmore church and
take the A417 toward Gloucester. After about a mile, the
entrance to castle and gardens is on the right.
Current opening (may vary):
April to May, Tuesday to Sundays, 10.30am to 5.00pm
June to August, daily, 10.30am to 5.00pm
September to October, 10.30am to 5.00pm
The castle is used for weddings so may not always be open.

The castle was built by Sir Rowland Leinthall in the fifteenth century, allegedly
with money obtained by ransoming French knights captured at Agincourt.
However, Rowland's wife, Margaret Fitzallan, was the grand-daughter of the
extremely wealthy Earl of Arundel, a relative of the king.

The entrance tower had a 'little pool' or reservoir on top, fed with water from
neighbouring hills. The castle was never built to be anything other than a home,
as Robinson states, the effect is 'collegiate rather than military' even though the
main gate had a portcullis. Sir Rowland died in 1450 and his daughter Elizabeth,
married to Thomas Cornewall, Baron of Burford, inherited it, but in 1510 her
grandson sold it to Sir Humphry Coningsby, Justice of the King's Bench, whose
family remained there for three centuries from 1510 to 1810. Their coat of
arms – three 'coneys' or rabbits – can be seen in several places. The large dining
room is known as the Coningsby Hall, even though most of it was built by the
Arkwrights who were here from 1810 to 1912. The Arkwright's main dining
hall is Victorian and has a portrait of Margaret, Countess of Coningsby.

Hampton Court chapel pulpit or 'ambo' (opposite)

The entire castle is home to the Van Kampen collection of arms and armour, including a knight on horseback and a stuffed lion which may not be to everyone's taste. Upstairs, two bedrooms were prepared for King William III and Queen Mary, one in red for the king and one in blue for the queen but it is not known if the royal visit every took place. Thomas Coningsby, whom William created Lord Coningsby of Clanbrassil in Ireland, took part in William's campaign in Ireland and was with the king at the Battle of the Boyne. The day before the battle, William's party were close to the riverbank when an enemy cannon opened up and a cannon ball bounced across the grass just brushing William's shoulder. Thomas had just moved the king back a few minutes before and was able to treat the slight wound with a handkerchief. The latter was kept in the family of Thomas's grandson, Lord Essex, for many years. Thus it is not surprising that the family would have been very disappointed if the royal visit never took place.

In 1808, Lord Essex sold the estate to the Arkwrights (well-known in the world of weaving machinery) who were responsible for much of the re-ordering of the house by the amateur architect Charles Hanbury-Tracey (later Lord Sudely) as well as the Atkinsons, William and John, whose drawings came to light fairly recently. In 1912 the Arkwrights sold the castle to Mrs Burrell and she sold it on in 1924 to Viscountess Hereford. In 1972 it was obtained by Capt Hon Philip Smith and in 1975 purchased by George Hughes. In 1994 the Van Kampens purchased it and carried out many essential repairs putting in the armour and hangings. The Daleys have instituted the opening arrangements and wedding licence.

THE CHAPEL

The chapel dates from the original building and stands at the left hand (NE) corner of the building for those approaching the gatehouse, similar to Hartlebury. It is probably the oldest unspoilt room in the castle. Built for the Catholic Leinthalls it has little of its original glass, sold off in 1924, but it has seating for 50, is used for civil wedding ceremonies today and there is an unusual carved wooden ambo with a statue of King Henry VIII. Arthur Mee states that when the cathedral tower collapsed in 1786 some of the stained glass was re-housed in this chapel, but alas there is no sign of it today.

Hartlebury Castle

A few miles north of Worcester off the A449 to Kidderminster, the ancient palace of the Bishops of Worcester is, at present, on the market. Please contact the Hartlebury Castle Preservation Trust at Hartlebury Museum or telephone 01299 250416 for opening arrangements. Café in adjoining wing.

Bishop Canteloupe started to build the castle in 1225 and Bishop Giffard obtained a licence to complete it in 1268. What the visitor sees today is the seventeenth and early eighteenth century building designed by Wood of

Hartlebury Castle

Oxford for Bishop Hough. Only the moat, or part of it, remain of a defensive castle. During the Civil War, Cromwell used it as a prison for captive Royalists and after this it fell into decay. The entrance is in the south side, which forms the bishop's private residence. On the left of the entrance is the chapel, the saloon and the great hall with its huge fireplace and portraits of bishops, one of whom is Hugh Latimer who finished up on the fire with Cranmer and Ridley in the bloody reign of Queen Mary I.

Up the ancient staircase with ball-headed banisters (for bishops to practice confirmations perhaps?) is the fine library which has a wonderful collection of seventeenth and eighteenth century books collected by Bishop Hurd, whose portrait by Gainsborough looks down on the visitor. There are first editions by Bewick and others and, although not a lending library, university students come here to study this unique collection.

THE CHAPEL

Hartlebury Chapel

Designed by Henry Keene in 1748 from a much earlier building, it has fan vaulting based on Henry VII's chapel at Westminster Abbey and Gothic furnishings, a tripartite screen, a fretwork door to the antechapel and a gallery with two windows that open so those unable to get to the service can watch from above. Latimer appears on one of the John Rowell side windows and also in the east window by Pearce (1898). The chapel is still used for occasional services – as recently by the Prayer Book Society. The service wing of the castle belongs to the Worcester Museum Service.

Harvington Hall

Near Kidderminster, Worcestershire DY10 4LR
Telephone: 01562 777846
www.harvingtonhall.com
Owner: RC Archdiocese of Birmingham
Directions: On a minor road, half a mile NE of the A450
and A448 crossroads at Mustow Green.
Current opening (may vary):
March to October:, Saturday and Sunday
April to September, Wednesday to Sunday, 11.30am to 4.00pm

The Hall is an irregular medieval and Elizabethan brick house built with a moat surrounding some of it. It was the home of the Packingtons and in the 18th century the Throckmortons, who went from here to Coughton Court (previously described) They took the staircase with them so today's one is a replica. There are numerous priest hiding places in the house as the Packingtons were Roman Catholics. The Jesuit, Henry Garnet, had a servant, Owen, who was a master at making priest holes. He worked here and also at Hindlip House. It was in Hindlip that Owen and two other priests were captured and put to death after the Gunpowder Plot. Packington's other daughter Mary married Sir John Yate and when he died in 1659, Lady Yate moved from Essex where they had gone to escape the worst of the Civil War back to Harvington where she remained for a further 40 years. On her death, her grand-daughter, Mary Throckmorton, and Robert, her husband, demolished two sides of the courtyard and built a new chapel in the top of the malt-house. The house became a girl's school after Sir Robert and Mary moved to Buckland in Devon. After this it seems to have been bailiffs and chaplains who lived her until 1923 when Mrs Ferris, mother of the late Lord Harvington, gave it to the Roman

Catholic diocese who own it today. Repaired in 1930 and again in 1985, it has some interesting wall paintings, very little furniture but is worth seeing for its priest holes and history.

THE GEORGIAN CHAPEL

Approached by a brick outside staircase, the upper floor was made into a chapel in 1743. In 1823 it was damaged by fire and the altar today has a piece of the altar stone in the centre. Above the altar is a seventeenth century Virgin and Child by, or after Baroccio. On the left of the door is a school desk and the registers of 1893-4 with a photograph of a teacher and school dated 1900, for after the fire the village school moved in until 1913. In 1986 it was restored as the chapel again and is used from time to time. The Church of St Mary's (1825) was built for Sir George Throckmorton with an adjoining Priest's House, joining the nave and set in the Elizabethan garden. This must have been pleasant for visiting priests who once had to endure damp, cold and vermin in the priest's room in the Hall.

Harvington Hall Priest's Room *(with drops of blood-patterned wallpaper)*

Harvington Hall, 1939, by William A Green *(opposite)*

Hawkstone Hall

Marchamley, Shrewsbury, Shropshire SY4 5LG
Telephone 0151 737 4710)   www.hawkstone-hall.com
Owners: The Redemptorist Congregation (The Redemptorists, Bishop Eton, Liverpool, L16 8NQ. Currently open only for guided tours during the summer. Coach parties welcome. Tea provided. Large grounds open separately.

This house was built between 1720-1750 for Sir Richard Hill, the deputy paymaster of the forces of King William III. One of his ancestors had been Lord Mayor of London. The original house was built in Palladian style with nine bays, wings and five-bay apsed pavilions. Much work on the house was done by Wyatt in 1832 who added a ballroom and conservatory.

In 1896 Lord Marchamley became the new owner and made more changes in 1906. Finally the Redemptorists added a new chapel before the war and an accommodation block in 1962, to the north-east. Visitors are shown the magnificent saloon, which is supposed to have been decorated by Flitcroft, which has a large painting of the Siege of Namur with Marlborough present alongside Hill. There is a ballroom which leads into Wyatt's conservatory, with a long vista from here to the statue of the Lord Mayor.

THE CHAPEL

Visitors are taken up some polished marble stairs to a room which is used as a chapel today. This, however, is not the cruciform brick-built chapel built separately from the house (in 1931) by G B Cox. Maybe when our group called the Redemptorists were using their chapel and we were shown this room instead. There was a careful guide who only took our party to certain rooms. However, the house seems to be used for retreats throughout the year and is a busy place.

Hawkstone Hall and Chapel *(right)*

Hawkstone Hall Chapel

The 1931 chapel, designed by G B Cox, a Birmingham architect, stands to the right hand side of the Hall, a large building in classic-Byzantine style with a green copper-topped turret and some nice wooden panelling inside. It has outside stairs but they are rarely used as the side entrance and passage connect easily with the main entrance of the Hall.

Inside there are comfortable chairs for 60, an organ (not working) and when we called a guitar perched up near the crossing place. The Cox altar has been removed and a square wooden one stands forward with a white tabernacle designed by Tim Hemington in 2000. It shows a 'dramatic approach of the Blessed Sacrament like an apocalypse'. There is also a cross based on the Italian cross at Arezzo St Dominic. It has been built by R H Brasier, a coachmaker who has worked at Canterbury Cathedral. The chapel is used very regularly and one hopes that someone will climb the vertical ladder and resurrect the organ.

Heath Chapel

Directions: Take the A49 to Craven Arms, turn off on B4368 to Diddlesbury then right through Peaton and Bouldon and when you reach Upper Heath Farm the key is in the porch with the wellington boots. Retrace your steps by 300 yards and the little chapel (or church as there is a graveyard nearby and a service once a year) stands alone in a field.

Heath Chapel is a Norman building, with plain nave and chancel: inside are box pews and remains of a wall painting. There is a brass to Rev Algernon Oldham, Archdeacon of Ludlow, who carefully restored the building in 1898 and preached his last sermon here in 1912. There are some small Norman windows, an outside string course, a font that may have come from elsewhere, three small seats at the back (perhaps for children) remains of hat pegs, a small harmonium from Chicago: when we called we were two days late for the August service.

Heath Chapel

It stands on the site of a medieval village which had a moated manor house nearby that now can only be identified by some mounds. Maybe it was built as the chapel for the owners of this house as even for a village church it seems remarkably small. *Don't forget to replace the key in the porch of the farmhouse even if you are afraid of dogs.*

Honington Hall

Nr Shipston-on-Stour, Warwickshire CV36 5AA
Owner: Ben Wiggin
Directions: Take A3400 towards Stratford-on-Avon and follow sign to Honington on right. House open to groups.
Telephone: 01608 661434. Church is next door.

The word 'Honington', in Domesday 'Hunitone', is supposed to be 'Homestead with honey (production)' so it must have had lime trees or flowers suitable for bees. The manor was one of the endowments of the Benedictine Priory of Coventry which was founded in 1403 by Leofric and his well-known wife, Lady Godiva. It passed to the Gibbs family but the present house was built by Henry Parker, a lawyer from the Inner Temple, who purchased the estate in 1670 and the architect of the present house is unknown. William Stanton, who built Denham Place, in Buckinghamshire, during the same period, has been suggested, but when the house passed to Joseph Townsend, his grandson, who married an heiress daughter of John Gore, MP for Grimsby, the house was enlarged. This work was done by either Sanderson Miller, who certainly worked on the grounds as landscape architect or by the Hiorns from Warwick who worked with Miller. The remarkable octagonal saloon is probably the finest room of its kind in Warwickshire. It was designed by an amateur, John Freeman, for £600, of which £100 was for a little carving. The pale blue walls make the very considerable carvings stand out clearly and even for the 1750's one wonders if it did not cost more than this.

ALL SAINTS, HONINGTON

Next door to Honington Hall, but can be approached from the village separately, All Saints church is a classical building dating from the 1680's and is full of the Parker and Townsend monuments. The coat of arms of the Stewarts looks down on the west end where there is a large monument to Sir Henry Parker and his son, who predeceased him.

Two of the Townsend monuments are by Westmacott, while in the south aisle is Lady Elizabeth's tomb, with its cherub described by Mee as 'a nightmare of a sculpture'. There are four hatchments and, of the six bells, three date from 1687. Outside, near the entrance, is the grave of Mary Elizabeth Townsend, founder of the Girls Friendly Society which, formed in 1875, still exists today.

Langley Chapel

Nr Acton Burnell, Shropshire
Telephone: 01926 852078   www.english-heritage.org.uk
Owner: English Heritage.
Open at all times. Service once a year, usually in September.

Langley Chapel, built about 1313 and repaired many times was mostly rebuilt by Sir Humphrey Lee, who had a house nearby, of which only the Gatehouse and chapel remain.

The Lee family, many of them Sheriffs of Shropshire, had strong connections with Moreton Corbet and Acton Burnell. Sir Humphrey, who rebuilt Langley Chapel, was a lawyer and became Sheriff in 1600. He was the first Shropshire man to be created baronet by King James I in 1620. Langley Hall fell into a ruinish state as Humphrey's son was a cavalier who lost heavily with fines and sequestrations in the Civil War. His eldest daughter Rachael married Ralph Cleaton and they lived at Lea Hall, which was purchased by the Mayalls in the 1920s and still survives. Langley Hall was demolished in the 1870's.

THE CHAPEL

The original chapel may date to the fourteenth century, but the earliest datestone is 1564, and the date 1601 is carved on one of the roofbeams. The roof has arch-braced collar beam trusses, plastered walls with rose emblems and fleur-de-lys. The floor has some fine medieval tiles with interesting patterns. The furnishings are a mixture of Laudian and Puritan fittings. There is a mobile wooden pulpit, a high pew for musicians, benches around the altar which seem to be grouped round for the elders, a communion rail on three sides, box pews and rough benches as in many

Welsh churches and a reader's desk. The Vicar used the moveable pulpit at the service I attended and at one point I thought he would pick it up and move during his sermon but it was probably to avoid the wasp that also attended the service.

Langley is well worth a visit. The ghost of Sir Humphrey would no doubt be pleased to see it in such fine condition.

Longworth Chapel of St James

Frome Court, Bartestree, Hereford HR1 4DX www.hct.org.uk
Opening Arrangements: Key kept in the Hospice. The chapel is owned by the Historic Chapels Trust, who are slowly restoring it. A blessing service was held in September 2010 attended by the Abbot of Belmont and the Hospice Chaplain.

Longworth Chapel, by Greg Brunt (above)

Langley Chapel (opposite)

This little chapel has had an amazing history. Originally built in the late fourteenth century, it has been used by Roman Catholics for over 600 years. Today it stands proudly next to the apartments now known as Frome Court, but up to 1995 the Convent of our Lady of Refuge at Caen.

It did not start out in its present position. The owner of the Longworth Estate in Bartestree in Victorian times was Robert Biddulph Phillipps, who was converted to Catholicism in 1851, his wife and two daughters the following year. He restored the chapel and in September 1859 mass was celebrated again. Two years before this, his daughter became a nun, joining the French order of the Sisters of Our Lady in Caen. After his wife's death in 1852, he wanted to endow a convent for his daughter: the sisters decided on higher ground, so it was built just off the Ledbury Road. The designer was E W Pugin. Iin 1863 his daughter and other sisters moved in. It became a home for hundreds of young girls suffering from deprivation. In 1864, however, Robert died and in his will he left orders that the chapel would be moved next to the convent. Since the late fourteenth century the chapel had been standing in a part of Hereford which suffers from floods as it is close to where the rivers Wye and Lugg meet. The chapel had fallen into disrepair and was being used as a mortuary chapel and barn. In 1869 it was finally removed stone by stone and rebuilt in its present site, dedicated to St James and the two marble moments to Elizabeth and Mary Anne Phillipps were erected. The whole move cost a mere £547.

Alas, the convent closed down in 1995 along with the chapel. The vandals moved in, windows were smashed and a fire broke out in 2002. Only a call to the Fire Brigade from the Hospice saved the building from complete destruction. An extra wall between the chapel and the convent was built and in 2010 it was purchased by the Historic Chapels Trust, still dedicated to St James, but now interdenominational and to be used as a spiritual and pastoral resource by the Hospice as well as a communal centre for inhabitants of Frome Court.

NB. See appendix for details of the Historic Chapels Trust.

The Lord Leycester Hospital

The Lord Leycester Hospital

Warwick CV8 4BH   www. lordleycester.com
Current opening (may vary): Tuesday to Sunday, 10.00 to 5.00pm
Garden open from April to September, 10.00am to 4.30pm
(4.00pm in winter).

Similar in purpose to the Coningsby Hospital in Hereford, built for 'the housing and maintenance of the needy, infirm or aged, nowadays for the ex-servicemen of which there are seven installed'. The Earl of Leicester founded it in 1571 for old soldiers who had been disabled in the reign of Elizabeth I in the building which was already 150 years old. Next door to the yard is the part of the Guildhall that has been taken over by the Museum of the Queen's Own Hussars and in the Chaplain's Dining Room is the history of how the regiment moved from horses to tanks.

The Guildhall, built by Richard Neville (Warwick the Kingmaker) (1450), was used by the Guilds until they were dissolved by King Henry VIII. Today members and their wives have self-contained flats although there is a communal restaurant (open to the visitor) and, if you are lucky, the Master's Garden is open and is a haven of peace in a town that suffers from continuous traffic. Note the face on a tree and an ancient Egyptian urn believed to be Roman in origin.

The courtyard and gallery have coats of arms of the main families associated with the Hospital: De Lisle, Dudley, Malpas, Gray, Beaumont, Ferrers, Sidney and Valance. The porcupine is the Sidney emblem and when Robert Dudley died in 1588 he left no heir, but in his will he left his property to Sir Philip Sidney of Penshurst Place, Kent and since then the De Lisles have been the Hereditary Patrons of the Hospital. One of the Sidneys was Master General of Ordnance at the end of the seventeenth century. He used his broad arrow badge rather than the porcupine, to be stamped on stores, powder kegs etc – a practice still in use today.

THE WEST GATE CHAPEL

Up the steps from the Hospital is the West Gate Chapel, still used by the Hospitallers for 9.30 prayers. It is mostly a Victorian building today as it was restored in 1860 by Sir George Gilbert Scott. Originally it was a chantry chapel for the Earl of Leicester who laid down the wording of the prayers used (every day except on Mondays). There is some stained glass by Clayton & Bell and above the south door a Morris window. William Morris was also responsible for the altar hangings. In 1694 most of medieval Warwick was destroyed in a dangerous fire. The Hospital was saved, however, and the recent Victorian additions, like the many plaster bears with ragged staffs, have saved the range of buildings from falling into ruin. Don't forget to see the Millennium knot garden which has a metal Warwick bear and staff.

Madresfield Court

Madresfield, Malvern, Worcestershire WR13 5AH
Telehone: 01684 579947.   www.elmley.org.uk
Owners: Trustees of the Madresfield Estate
Directions: Two miles NE of Malvern off the Worcester Road
No public opening in 2012 due to refurbishment: Visits from
2013 by advance appointment only. Tours may be held on
occasional dates between April and July: early booking will be
essential. Garden and arboretum.

Madresfield today is a Victorian Gothic moated building, designed by
P C Hardwick in 1865. The Bell Tower was added in 1875. There was
a medieval hall which in Tudor times became a manor house and later a
long gallery was installed. The Lygon family who inherited the house
from William de Bracy in the thirteenth century have been here ever since.
During the Civil War the Lygons, without much enthusiasm, supported
Parliament and apart from a brief problem when the Royalists occupied
the house in 1651, the house remained unscathed unlike Brampton Bryan.

William Lygon inherited a lot of money as godson to King William
III. Lygon became Baron Beauchamp of Powycke and by 1815 he was
an Earl. It was the Fifth Earl who reconstructed the house and the
sixth Earl, a very religious man, who constructed the chapel off the
library. The Seventh Earl supported the Arts and Crafts movement and
was responsible for bringing in some interesting stained glass, a lattice
window designed by B. Lamplugh and an Arts and Craft lamp by Ashbee.
In the staircase hall with its gallery there is a large picture 'The Quarries
of Syracuse' by none other than Edward Lear (1853) and a picture of the
entire family by Ranken, painted in 1924 on the occasion of Viscount
Elmley's 21st birthday.

It was recently revealed that Madresfield was to be the bolt hole of King George VI, Queen Elizabeth and their two daughters in 1940 if the Germans had landed. They would not have remained long because their route to Liverpool was planned, with probably another stop at a house in Cheshire. There would have only just been enough bedrooms for the royal party and in the house is a list of who was to occupy them. There is a muniments room with estate surveys, accounts, regimental details from Waterloo and other interesting documents. Evelyn Waugh based *Brideshead Revisited* on Madresfield as he knew the family well. One of his other novels, *Black Mischief*, was dedicated to the Lygon daughters.

Madresfield Court, by Alison Poole

Madresfield Court chapel fresco detail *(opposite)*

THE CHAPEL

Not always open, the chapel is a mass of colour. The wife of the seventh Earl dedicated the chapel, with its Arts and Crafts painted walls, in 1902 as a wedding present to her husband, the Seventh Earl. The Birmingham Group of artists and craftsmen were called in. Frescoes were painted by Henry Payne and his three assistants. The Gaskins, husband and wife, made the altar cross and the chalice and paten are by Robert Hilton. William Bidlake designed the triptych and Charles Gerl designed the altar frontal. The family were High Church Anglicans (like Evelyn Waugh) and employed a resident chaplain. Today the chapel is not often used except for very special occasions.

Of all the private chapels in this book, Madresfield is by far the finest, although the over decoration must have been a great distraction especially for visitors trying to concentrate on the chaplain's sermon. It seats about twelve.

Moreton Corbet Castle

Moreton Corbet Castle, Shropshire   Telephone 01926 852078
Open all year.   www.english-heritage.org.uk
Owner: English Heritage, for the Corbet family.
Directions: Seven miles NE of Shrewsbury off the B5063.

The ruined castle, roughly triangular in shape, was built by the Toret family in about 1200 and inherited by marriage in 1329 by the Corbets. In spite of being a ruin today, it is worth a visit. The gatehouse has the Corbet crest and initials of Sir Andrew Corbet, 1579, and an elephant and castle, supposed to come not from London, but from the Scottish family of Oliphants, captured by one of the Corbets in a Scottish battle. Sir Andrew added the great hall with large mullion windows and fireplaces. This encroached on the moat which had to be filled in and when Sir Andrew died in 1578 the building was

Moreton Corbet Castle

unfinished and still in this state when his son Robert, who had travelled in Italy appeared to add his Italian tastes to the building, which Pevsner states would have compared with Somerset House in the Strand or Longleat; alas, Robert died of the plague in 1583 with the work still incomplete.

During the Civil War, the castle was garrisoned by Sir Vincent Corbet for the King, but Shropshire had many Parliamentarian supporters and on September 10th, 1644, a force under Lord Calvin and Colonel Reinkling from Wem approached at night. They made no attempt to approach by stealth but Reinkling sent his drummers to different points and issued orders to imaginary regiments in a loud voice. After a window had been forced and some grenades exploded, Corbet surrendered with his 80 foot and 30 horse. After the war, Sir Vincent had to sell land to pay his fines and little could be done to repair the castle. The Corbets struggled on until the nineteenth century when they purchased Preston Brockhurst which they then had to sell to Samuel Wingfield, builder of Preston Hall, but in 1843, Rowland Wingfield who lived at Onslow Hall, sold Preston back to the Corbet family and there they still live.

THE CHURCH

Originally a chapel and a subsidiary of St Mary's, Shawbury, St Bartholemew's church dates from the 12th century with the south aisle added 1330-40 and other additions in the seventeenth and eighteenth centuries. In 1904, Sir Ninian Comper added a heraldic tester over the altar, reredos and other fittings. Naturally there are many Corbet tombs and the Chancel is dedicated to Vincent Stuart Corbet who died in 1904 when a schoolboy at Eton. The east window is dated 1892 and is in memory of Vincent Rowland Corbet and faces in the window are of the family.

There is a Corbet pew on the south side, dated 1778 and its entrance is in place of a south window. The west window is in memory of Augusta Corbet, d.1838. In the south aisle is a tomb chest to Sir Robert and his wife, three sons and five daughters: he died in 1513 and she in 1563. A Corbet tomb (moved from Shawbury Church) shows Sir Richard Corbet and his wife (1567).

The raven, squirrel and elephant and castle are all evident here. Sir Vincent of Civil War fame has his monument in the south aisle and in the family vault are 14 members of the family. The vault had to be sealed in 1896 by Sir Walter Corbett as, according to the guide book, there was 'standing room only'.

Morville Hall

Near Bridgnorth, Shropshire WV16 5NB
Owner: The National Trust   www.nationaltrust.org.uk
Opening Arrangements: Admission by guided tour, by written appointment only with the tenants.
Please contact Dr and Mrs C. Douglas directly.

Moreton Corbet Church - Corbet tomb, 1567 *(opposite)*

Morville Hall by Ascott Davies

Unlike most National Trust houses, Morville has no shop, tea room or roped off interiors. This is really a private house which was given by the last owner, Miss Audrey Bythell, to the National Trust in 1966 along with 140 acres, mostly of farmland.

The Georgian facade that greets you, with a 'U' shaped house and its two wings connected by high pillared walls in grey stone facing the church across a large green, is one of the most delightful sights in Shropshire.

However, it is basically a Jacobean house you see. Morville was a Saxon site: the church is mostly Norman and became a Benedictine Priory under the Abbot of Shrewsbury. In 1546, after the Dissolution, it was purchased by Roger Smyth, MP for Bridgnorth, and he and his son George constructed an E-shaped Jacobean house with turret stairs left and right (which still exist). In 1642, George's grandson was killed fighting for his king at Edgehill and the house passed by marriage to Arthur Weaver of Montgomeryshire. A century further on and another Arthur Weaver commissioned William Baker to Georgianise the house. He added the pavilions, inserted oak panelling and added giant pilasters and columns on the front. He is best known for his Butter Cross in Ludlow and the two buildings share some features. The top floor and porch with its pediment were added by Arthur Blayney, a cousin, who succeeded to Morville in 1762. The picture of the house in the eighteenth century shows the pepperpots and chimneys with the Weaver and Blayney families on the lawn. The original belongs to HM Government and this is just a copy. At the time of Waterloo, Morville was acquired by Frederick Acton of Aldenham, nearby, who let it out to tenants, the rent being £170 a year in 1875. Joseph Warren died, aged 90, having taken the lease then. His daughter lived a long time, dying in 1928 at the age of 85.

Morville Hall and St Gregory's Church *(opposite)*

Great structural alterations were made by H S Bayliss, a cinema owner, who bought Morville in 1930 and removed the Victorian library and main staircase, both behind the hall, replacing it with a loggia used by the family today. However, the lack of a main stair makes it unsuitable for National Trust parties which is a blessing for the tenant who is a furniture enthusiast and also looks after the large garden. Unlike some houses in the area – Shipton and Upton Cresset – there is little plaster ceiling decoration except in the kitchen (called the winter parlour by Pevsner) where the same plasterer (c.1580) has been at work as at Upton Cressett and Wilderhope (a youth hostel). In 1936 the house was sold to the Bythells of Cheshire and their daughter lived here during the war and afterwards in 'genteel poverty' leaving much to be done by the new tenant and the National Trust.

ST GREGORY'S CHURCH

The church was built in the twelfth century but, as Mr Leonard points out, with the nave and chancel first, then the tower, and last of all the aisles. In the chancel is some fine fourteenth century glass showing Christ crucified and the font, a Norman tub-shaped one, has some wonderful carvings including at least one human face.

There is a monument to Sir George Acton (1716) and other Aldenham monuments to Actons in the graveyard along with about three Bythell graves. The priest's doorway includes a tablet of 1683 and the initials AWI 1683, possibly Arthur Weaver and his wife, or Arthur Weaver first, with a small tympanum showing an oak tree. The clock, which still chimes every quarter-hour, was given to the tower by the Misses Warren in memory of their parents. So, although St Gregory's is a parish church in Hereford diocese, it is still looked upon as belonging to the Hall.

St Gregory's Church Morville Hall font carving *(opposite)*

Moseley Old Hall

Near Wolverhampton WV10 7HY   Telephone: 01902 782808
Owner: The National Trust   www.nationaltrust.org.uk
Directions: Take the A449 from centre of Wolverhampton,
go under motorway, take turning right to Moseley Hall on
right. Go past this and turn left to find the Old Hall. Current
opening (may vary):
3 March to 1 July, 12 to 5.00pm, Wednesday, Saturday,
Sunday. 2 July to 9 September, 12 to 5pm, all week
except Thursdays and Fridays. 12 September to 31
October, 12 to 5pm, Wednesday, Saturday, Sunday.
7 November to 16 December, 12 to 4.00pm, Sundays only.
Tea shop, garden, shop, display of Charles II history.

Moseley is now a brick building but inside is much like the original farmhouse
where King Charles II came after his spell in the Oak Tree (see Boscobel).
He was escorted by William Penderel and found Lord Wilmot at Moseley,
a Catholic house and home of Thomas Whitgreave, and his priest, Father
Huddleston, who had three students with him who acted as lookouts from
the third floor windows. The farmhouse overlooked the road and many
Scots passed by en route for home after losing their battle with Cromwell at
Worcester. September 1651 was not a happy time for Royalists. Charles was
described on his arrival there in September 1651 as:

On his head a long white steeple-crowned hat, without any lining other than grease,
both sides of the brim so doubled with handling they looked like two spouts; a
leather doublet full of holes and half black with grease about the sleeves, collar and
waist; an old green woodreeve's coat, threadbare and patched in most places, with
a pair of breeches of the same cloth and in the same condition, the flaps hanging

Moseley Old Hall Chapel *(opposite)*

down to the middle of his legs; hose and shoes of different parishes; the hose was grey much darned and clouted, especially about the knees, under which he had a pair of flannel riding-stockings of his own with tops cut off. His shoes had been cobbled with leather patches both on the soles and seams, and the upper-leathers so cut and slashed, to adapt them to his feet, that they could no longer defend him either from water or dirt. This exotic and deformed dress added to his short hair by the ears, his face coloured brown by walnut leaves ... he scarcely became discernable who he was, even to those before acquainted with his person.

It was given out that Father Huddleston had a Catholic friend staying and the servants were all sent on errands, except the cook who was a Catholic. Luckily Wilmot knew that Colonel Lane, one of his officers, had a pass for his sister to go to Bristol with a servant from his house five miles away at Bentley. Soldiers arrived on Tuesday afternoon and the King was hurriedly put in the priest hole, a cupboard with a trap door, but they had come to question Mr Whitgrave who had not been at Worcester and was able to prove this. Luckily the next day Wilmot – who had left to see the Colonel before the enemy soldiers arrived – returned with horses so the King left, re-dressed by the Colonel in a country suit as worn by a farmer's son, given £20 and mounted with Jane Lane. She sat side-saddle behind him and, escorted by Wilmot, set out for the west country where, with more adventures, he eventually got to Sussex and onto a coal ship for France.

The house contains a brew-house, buttery, Mr Whitgreave's room, a study and in the attic, apart from the chapel, there is a little room for making rosewater and other herbal lotions. Downstairs there is a parlour, dining room and a very busy kitchen.

THE CHAPEL

Also known as the Oratory, it now consists of six stools with seating for a dozen and a small altar with a Spanish crucifix. The chapel was licensed in 1791 and used regularly so that the cross and other tell-tale

Moseley Old Hall hiding place *(opposite)*

objects didn't have to be hidden away. When Charles was restored to the throne he rewarded Jane Lane, giving her a jewel worth £1000, the sum that Cromwell would have given for his capture when on the run to an informant. Father Huddleston was the priest who came to him on his deathbed and converted him to Catholicism.

Moseley has a lot of character and no student of King Charles II and his escape after Worcester should miss it, as well as those who are interested in the life of simple farmers of the seventeenth century.

Rotherwas Court Chapel

Rotherwas, Hereford
Owner: English Heritage
www.english-heritage.org.uk
Open at any reasonable time
in daylight hours.
Key from nearby garage
Directions: 1½ miles SE of
Hereford on B4399.
Very close to the
Household Waste Site
(see brown road signs).

Rotherwas Chapel by Alison Poole

Rotherwas Room as rebuilt in Herbert Pratt's Long Island mansion

Rotherwas Room today

Rotherwas was mentioned in Domesday, when it belonged to Gilbert Fitz Tyrold. At the time of Edward I, it belonged to Richard de Welles, who had two hides here of William de la Bere. However, it was acquired in the middle of the fifteenth century by the Bodenhams of Much Dewchurch and became their main seat. It is described by Blount in 1678 as:

> ... *a delicious seat, situate near the river Wye, within two miles of Hereford, abounding with stores of excellent fruit and fertile arable land, having also a park within less than half a mile of the house, where there is a neat lodge upon the hill which overlooks the whole country adjacent'. The house is built partly of old timber work but one end of it was new built of stone in the last age by Sir Roger Bodenham (who was knighted by King James I and married Bridget, daughter of Humphrey Baskerville of Eardisley). There is a fair parlour full of coats of arms and a dining room wainscoted with walnut trees, and on the mantel tree of the chimney twenty-five coats in one achievement, with the motto 'Veritas Liberabit'.*

The chapel is all that remains today. During the Civil War the house was captured by Parliamentary troops, the outhouses ruined and Roger Bodenham, a defender of Hereford, became a Knight of the Royal Oak at the Restoration. They were Roman Catholics and the dining room, described above, was dismantled in 1913 and sold in the New York showrooms of Charles Duveen. Here it was purchased by Herbert Pratt (of Standard Oil) for his house in Long Island, but he changed his mind and donated it to his old college, Amherst in Massachusetts, including the 1611 chimneypiece, where it stands today in all its splendour. It was incorporated into the Mead building at the college in 1948-49, where it is open to the public. As the late King James I is supposed to have said, 'Everyone may not live at Rotherwas', punning the ancient saying about Corinth. Robinson says that on dewy mornings the foundations of the old mansion (it was mostly rebuilt in 1731) can still be seen, near the chapel which has just been restored by the Hereford architects Hook Mason (2010).

Rotherwas Room coat of arms above the fireplace

Rotherwas Room carving detail in maple panelling

Shipton Hall

Much Wenlock, Shropshire TF13 6JZ   Telephone: 01746 87225
Directions: Situated on the B4378 Ludlow to Much Wenlock road.
Current opening (may vary):
Thursdays, 2.30pm to 5.30pm (also same hours on Sundays
and Mondays of bank holiday weekends)

This is a family home complete with dovecote, farm office, a few horses and a large garden. For the compulsive shopper there is also a materials (curtains and wallpaper etc) shop in one of the barns which makes a nice change from the usual National Trust shop.

The house is basically Elizabethan and was built in or around 1587 by Richard Lutwyche at the time of the marriage of his daughter to Thomas Mytton. The Myttons were here for over 300 years and the Bishops for only about 80 years. The Elizabethan symmetry of an 'H' shaped building is broken by the porch being made into a tower of four storeys looking South East where the village once stood – the Myttons removed it apart from the pub. Thomas Pritchard, designer of the Iron Bridge in Coalbrookdale, was called in to Georgianise the rooms in a mixture of Rococco, Gothic and Palladian designs. Only the Elizabethan panelling over the hall in the ladies' sewing room remains. It was in this room that 19-year-old Harriott was locked up one day in 1792 to stop her running off with wealthy local Thomas More of Larden Hall (demolished in 1968), who was much older than her. Harriott spent the time writing a message to her friend Ann on the window pane for all in the house to read, but one wonders how Ann was supposed to read it:

By Dint of times this argument Ann learned,
Who'd be happy must be unconcerned
Must all her assets in her bosom wear

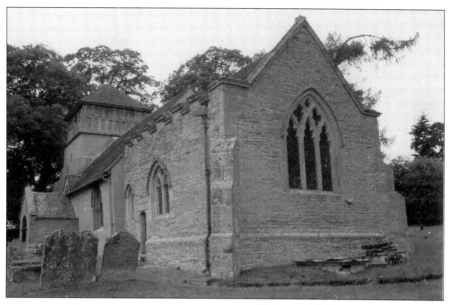

St James Church Shipton Hall

And seek for peace and comfort only there.
Harriott Mytton December 18 1792

Fortunately in the church is the monument to the couple and we read that Harriott outlived her husband by many years, dying in 1851 aged 78. She must have been a lady of great fortitude and determination.

The house has some fine pictures and china, but personally I like best the 1956 painting by Lionel Edwards of Mrs Bishop's mother-in-law on her favourite horse riding close to Shipton; it certainly deserves its pride of place in the main hall.

THE CHURCH

In the grounds of the Hall, St James Church is basically Norman with a chancel rebuilt by John Lutwych in 1589, the windows retaining their thirteenth century appearance – the stonework being renewed in 1905-6.

There is a monument to Mary Mytton 1640 and five wall monuments in the chancel to Mytton who died between 1770 and 1864.

However, it is the connection with the *Mayflower*, 1620, for which the church is forever famous. Samuel More and his wife Katherine were married in the church, their four children baptized in the font there, but Samuel thought they were the result of the adultery of his wife with a local farmer, Jacob Blakeway. Legal proceedings followed and Samuel obtained a divorce. He was friendly with a group of puritans who were sailing for the New World on the Mayflower so he put all four children in their care and all four arrived in New Plymouth – Ellen, Jasper, Richard and Mary. The first winter, though, with its intense cold, lack of food and 'periles and miseries' killed off all but one of the children – Richard – who was to live until his eighties.

His guardians, the Brewsters, put him to work aged six as a bird scarer, reed gatherer and nail maker for their plank houses. He was 14 when his name appeared in the 1627 census and he must have returned to England as his name appears on the passenger list of the *Blessing* from London in 1635. Also on the ship was a young girl of the same age, Christian Hunter. They married the following year and moved to Salem. He was granted some land and by the 1650's was the owner of a ketch. He and Christian had seven children, one of whom died in infancy. His wife died aged 60 and Richard married Jane Crumpton, widow of Sam Crumpton, who had been killed in an Indian ambush. When he was 60, Richard retired from the sea, keeping a half share in the *Swan*, a trading vessel. He died in 1692 according to his gravestone, at the age of 84. However, a deed has been found, dated 1696, transferring land 'bought of Richard More of Salem lately deceased'. The unwanted child from Shipton thus became the longest living survivor of the *Mayflower* and his gravestone, even if the date is dubious, the only know gravestone of a passenger of the *Mayflower*.

Stokesay Castle

Craven Arms, Shropshire SY7 9AH   Telephone: 01588 672544
Owner: English Heritage   www.english-heritage.org.uk
Current opening (may vary):
April to September, daily, 10.00am to 5.00pm
October, Wednesday and Sunday, 10am to 5.0pm
November to February, Thursday to Sunday, 10am to 4.00pm
March, Wednesday to Sunday, 10am to 5.00pm
Closed 24 to 26 December and 1 January
Shop and restaurant.

One of Britain's oldest houses, built by Laurence of Ludlow in 1290 (the church was already there) as a moated site which although moderately defensive was not strong enough to withstand a siege. The 1640 gatehouse of wood and containing an entrance for carts, seems to have strayed from the centre of Ludlow. There are small loopholes in the door. Perhaps an archer could use them, but why was there not a stone gatehouse when the Civil War was just about to start? In fact, Lord Craven who lived here then was a Royalist and surrendered to the Parliamentarians in 1645 without a shot being fired. There is a stained glass picture in Stokesay Court showing this event.

Opposite the gatehouse on the left is the tower with its lookout on the roof. There were hinged shutters on the windows which are now open to the wind and rain. The English Heritage notices are all about the five varieties of bat that have homes here. The nearby pond, no doubt a fish pond for the Ludlows, encourages bats. In 1830 a fire in the south tower destroyed many of the inner timbers but has not harmed the stonework.

ST JOHN THE BAPTIST, STOKESAY

Next door to the castle but outside the ramparts, the church one sees today is a seventeenth century rebuild as the original was largely destroyed during the Civil War.

Thus the nave is 1654 and the chancel 1664 with most of the fittings, including the magnificent squire's pew, dating from the Restoration period. The west gallery is of the same date. In 1683, a Mr Francis painted numerous wall paintings but, although conserved in 1988, they are not easy to make out.

The stained glass in the nave by Payne of Birmingham dates from 1903, and the window by Hogan, of the saints Michael and Gabriel, dates from 1913. It is difficult to see any connections with those who lived in the castle with the names on the monuments, as the church is now the parish church of Craven Arms. It is likely that during the Civil War the Cravens had their own chaplain and services inside the castle and only after the Restoration did they and the later owners of the castle move into the church.

Stoneleigh Abbey

Estate Office, Stoneleigh, Warwickshire CV8 2LF
Telephone: 01926 858535
www.stoneleighabbey.org
Owner: Stoneleigh Abbey Ltd
Current opening (may vary):
Tuesday to Thursday, Sundays and bank holidays
House tours at 11.00am, 1.00pm and 3.00pm (tours 1¼ hours)
Free Entry to grounds with English Heritage card (tour extra)
Tea shop and toilets in Orangery.
Small shop in the gatehouse.

Stokesay Castle and church

Stokesay Castle, by Alison Poole

Originally a Cistercian monastery, Stoneleigh became the home of the Leigh family at the Dissolution. The gatehouse, once the 'hospice' for visitors, is still intact, but the stone church was demolished after the Dissolution in 1536. Much of the medieval stonework has been incorporated into the house, although the Abbey was built in sandstone, similar to Kenilworth Castle. The new house was built by the Leighs who employed Smith of Warwick. He used a grey coloured stone that in no way matches the sandstone of the old abbey buildings. Smith's estimate was £545 for a three storey building excluding all scaffolding, trestles etc and removal of old walls etc and the rubbish which was all extra.

Smith's west wing is rather staid English baroque with the window pediments run into the windows above them and the repairs after the fire of the 1960's rather makes the stonework appear camouflaged. However, the inside is mostly magnificent so any house should not be judged on its outer appearance.

The first Lord Leigh, a London merchant and Lord Mayor, died in 1571 and his son Sir Thomas died in 1626. The next Lord Leigh, a Royalist, entertained King Charles I here and was fined by Parliament. It was Thomas and his son Edward who called in Smith to design the new house, finished in 1726. Edward married Mary Holbeach, a wealthy lady who was said to guard the purse strings. The Leighs seem to have made useful marriages for Thomas, fourth Lord Leigh, married into the Cravens who were wealthy neighbours. There is little furniture in Stoneleigh, but what there is (i.e. in the card room) is top quality. William Henry Leigh entertained Queen Victoria here with Prince Albert for two nights in 1858, William Henry Leigh died in 1905, aged 81, and the golden days of Stoneleigh were over.

There was a strong connection between the Leighs and the Austens and Jane writes of the house in *Mansfield Park*, called Sotherton in the book. The Bertrams, Crawfords, Mrs Norris and Fanny arrive at the house where after a cold meal in the dining room, Mrs Rushworth shows them:

… a number of rooms all lofty, and many large, and amply furnished in

Stoneleigh Abbey chapel ceiling *(opposite)*

the taste of 50 years back with shining floors, solid mahogany, rich damask, marble, gilding and carving … of the pictures there were abundance and some few good but a larger part were family portraits no longer anything to anybody but Mrs Rushworth … she could relate of the family in former times, its rise and grandeur, regal visits and loyal efforts… having visited more rooms than could be supposed to be of any other use than to contribute to the window tax and fine employment for housemaids. "Now," said Mrs Rushworth, "We are coming to the chapel, which properly we ought

Stoneleigh Abbey Gatehouse

to enter from above and look down upon (as today); but as we are among
friends I will take you in this way if you excuse me."
Mary Crawford and Fanny (or Jane) have a conversation about prayers.
"Now left off" says Mary, "Each generation has its improvements."

The park was originally planned by Repton, who illustrated his ideas in a
red book, but he was not in the end employed due to the death of Rev T
Leigh in 1813. Christopher Hussey reckons the Repton idea of moving
the river nearer the house was carried out by Henry Wise, royal gardener,
who lived at Warwick Priory. The cricket pitch in front of the west front
is used by the local Stoneleigh cricket club and there is a picture in the
house of Chandos Leigh, who was at Harrow, holding a cricket bat.

Today there are about 27 inhabitants of the house, all with their own
apartments, and the grounds are beautifully looked after. There appears to
be a new bridge under construction so nothing has yet been completed.
The saloon is used for corporate entertainment.

THE CHAPEL

The Leighs were high church and in the 1740's two rooms were turned
into the present chapel with some fine plasterwork by Wright and
a gallery accessible from the drawing room. The main saloon, which
escaped the fire, has plasterwork illustrating the Labours of Hercules.
Our guide said that the local church was very Hanoverian and rather low
church and the family preferred the Jacobite High Church services and
found a chaplain to come to their chapel. There have been exhibitions
of nineteenth century costumes in the chapel, one of which remained
when I visited. The chapel is licensed for weddings although only seating
about 80 persons. Jane Austen wrote Mansfield Park in 1806 and today
the chapel, though boasting a fine organ, is hardly ever used.

Upton Cressett Hall

Bridgnorth, Shropshire WV16 6UH   Telephone: 01746 714308
Website: www.uptoncressetthall.co.uk
Owner: Bill Cash MP
Current opening (may vary):
May to October, Thursdays, 2.30pm to 5.00pm
Parties by appointment

Originally a Roman site, Upton Cressett Hall was constructed in the fourteenth century and the gatehouse – now used as a self-let flat – in the 1580's by Richard Cressett, Sheriff of Shropshire, who also re-modelled the Hall, no doubt inserting the fine twisted chimneystacks. This would have been connected by a high wall to the house, which was moated, so that a fortified manor would have been created. The gatehouse still has stone slabs for carriages or carts to enter without jolting the inmates and there was a drawbridge between gatehouse and house. Edward Cressett in 1616 established a deer park and there are remains of fish ponds.

Hugh Cressett was a Lancastrian and Constable of Mortimer Castle and his son was a Yorkist lawyer and Sheriff of Shropshire, but was replaced by Gilbert Talbot after Bosworth (1485). Richard's son Edward was a member of Charles I's council and tried to rescue him from Carisbrooke in 1648. His grandson was James, who was Envoy Extraordinary to the Court of Hanover in the reign of William and Mary. Another Cressett played a part in the negotiations between government and during the madness of King George III. The present owners purchased the Hall from the Chapmans, and since 1971 have done much work, including the recently painted dining room and staircase by Adam Dart. This was commissioned by Mr Cash's son, who has recently moved into the house

Upton Cressett Hall and gatehouse

with his family. When we called there was an open air Shakespeare play about to be performed on the lawn. Being England in summer it was going to rain any minute!

ST MICHAEL'S CHURCH

This is a 12th century chapel just below the lawn (tennis court) which is now in the hands of the Churches Conservation Trust. The Norman chancel arch has four zig-zag mouldings and the south nave doorway also has a Norman arch with a chevron. There appears to have been a 13th century north aisle, demolished much later, as the arches can be seen both inside and outside the church. There was once a brass in the north wall but this has been transferred to Monkhopton, showing Richard Cressett and his wife Jane, two sons and three daughters in 1640. Until recently there were about four pews in the church and an occasional service was held, but these have gone.

Appendix: The Historic Chapels Trust

St George's German Lutheran Church, 55 Alie Street, London El 8EB
0207 4810533   www.hct.org.uk   chapels@hct.org.uk

The Historic Chapels Trust was established in 1993 to take into ownership redundant chapels and other places of worship in England which are of outstanding architectural importance and historic interest. The object is to secure their preservation, repair and maintenance for public benefit, including contents, burial grounds and ancillary buildings. There is a newsletter once or twice a year. Chapels currently owned by the Trust are:

- Bethesda Methodist Chapel, Stoke-on-Trent
- Biddlestone RC Chapel, Northumberland
- Chantry Chapel and Burial Ground, Essex
- Coanwood Friends Meeting House, Northumberland
- Cote Baptist Chapel, Oxfordshire
- Dissenters' Chapel, Kensal Green Cemetery, London
- Farfield Friends Meeting House, West Yorkshire
- Grittleton Strict Baptist Chapel, Wiltshire
- Longworth RC Chapel, Herefordshire *(see page 60)*
- Penrose Methodist Chapel, Cornwall
- St Benet's RC Chapel, Merseyside
- St George's German Lutheran Church, London
- Salem Chapel, Devon
- Shrine of Our Lady of Lourdes, Blackpool
- Todmorden Unitarian Church, West Yorkshire
- Umberslade Baptist Church, Solihull
- Wainsgate Baptist Church, West Yorkshire
- Wallasey Memorial Unitarian Church, Merseyside
- Walpole Old Chapel, Suffolk
- Westgate Methodist Chapel, Co Durham

St Michael's Upton Cressett *(opposite)*

Bibliography

Bearman, R (Ed), *Stoneleigh Abbey, The House, Its Owners, Its Land,* Stratford, 2004

Buchan, J, A *Book of Escapes and Hurried Journeys*, Edinburgh, 1922

Cook, G H, *Medieval Chantries and Chantry Chapels*, London, 1963

Forrest, H E, *Some Old Shropshire Houses and their Owners*, Shrewsbury, 1924

Kinross, J, *Discovering the Smallest Churches In England,* Stroud, 2008

Leonard, J, *Churches of Herefordshire and their Treasures,* Hereford, 2000

Leonard, J, *Churches of Shropshire and their Treasures*, Hereford, 2004

Mee, A, *Warwickshire, Shropshire, Herefordshire and Worcestershire*, London, 1938, 1942, 1948, 1950

Pevsner, N, & Newman, J, *Buildings of England: Shropshire*, London, 2006

Pevsner, N, *Buildings of England Series: Herefordshire*, London, 1963

Pevsner, N, & Wedgwood, A, *Buildings of England: Warwickshire*, London, 1966

Pevsner, N, *Buildings of England:* Staffordshire, London, 1974

Reid, P, *Burke & Savills Guide to Country Houses*, Vol 2, London, 1980.

Robinson, Rev C J, *A History of the Mansions and Manors of Herefordshire,* Hereford, 2009

Robinson, Rev C J, *A History of the Castles of Herefordshire and their Lords*, Hereford, 1872

Illustrations

Index

Rotherwas Chapel *(opposite)*

fineleaf

PUBLISHED BY FINELEAF, ROSS-ON-WYE
www.fineleaf.co.uk